The Ultimate Guitar Theory Chart

Introduction

The **Ultimate Guitar Theory Chart** has been created to assist you in learning basic music theory. It is a fast and fun way to gain instant access to essential interval, chord, scale, and key information.

Contents

- 2   Guitar Fingerboard Chart
- 3   Intervals
- 4   The Circle of Fifths
- 5   Major Scales
- 5   Natural Minor Scales
- 6   The Harmonized Major Scales
- 6   The Harmonized Natural Minor Scales
- 7   Chord Construction
- 8   Scale Construction

ISBN 978-1-4803-8512-2

Copyright © 2014 by HAL LEONARD CORPORATION
International Copyright Secured   All Rights Reserved

No part of this publication may be reproduced in any form or by any means without the prior written permission of the Publisher.

Visit Hal Leonard Online at
www.halleonard.com

Guitar Fingerboard Chart

Use the *Guitar Fingerboard Chart* below to help you quickly locate all the notes within the first twelve frets.

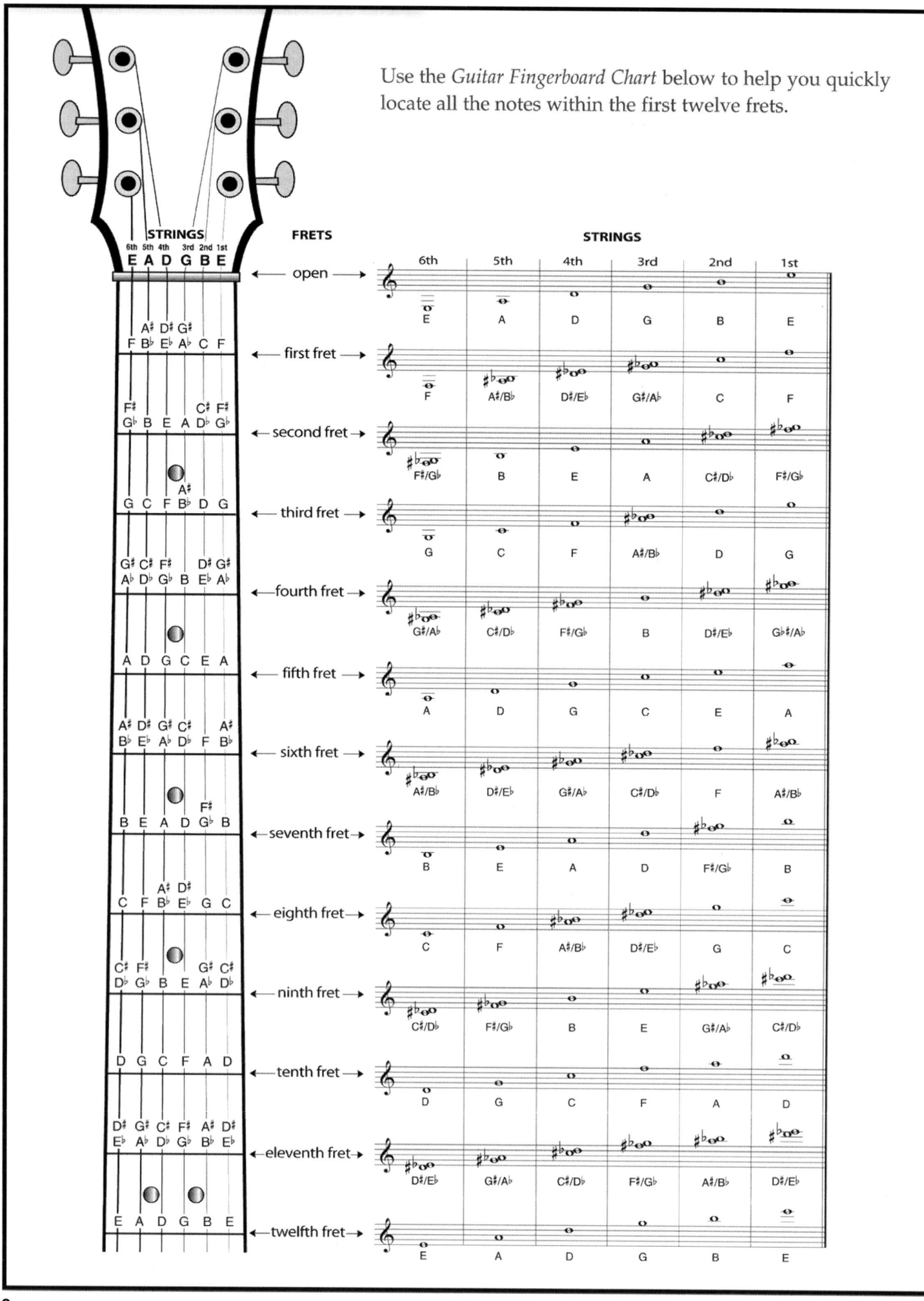

Intervals

INTERVAL	ABBREVIATION	STEPS	INTERVAL	ABBREVIATION	STEPS
UNISON	unis	none	MAJOR SIXTH	M6	4 1/2
MINOR SECOND	m2	half	AUGMENTED SIXTH	aug6	5
MAJOR SECOND	M2	whole	MINOR SEVENTH	m7	5
AUGMENTED SECOND	aug2	1 1/2	MAJOR SEVENTH	M7	5 1/2
MINOR THIRD	m3	1 1/2	PERFECT OCTAVE	P8	6
MAJOR THIRD	M3	2	MINOR NINTH	m9	6 1/2
PERFECT FOURTH	P4	2 1/2	MAJOR NINTH	M9	7
AUGMENTED FOURTH	aug4	3	AUGMENTED NINTH	aug9	7 1/2
DIMINISHED FIFTH	dim5	3	AUGMENTED ELEVENTH	aug11	9
PERFECT FIFTH	P5	3 1/2	MINOR THIRTEENTH	m13	10 1/2
AUGMENTED FIFTH	aug5	4	MAJOR THIRTEENTH	M13	11
MINOR SIXTH	m6	4			

The Circle of Fifths

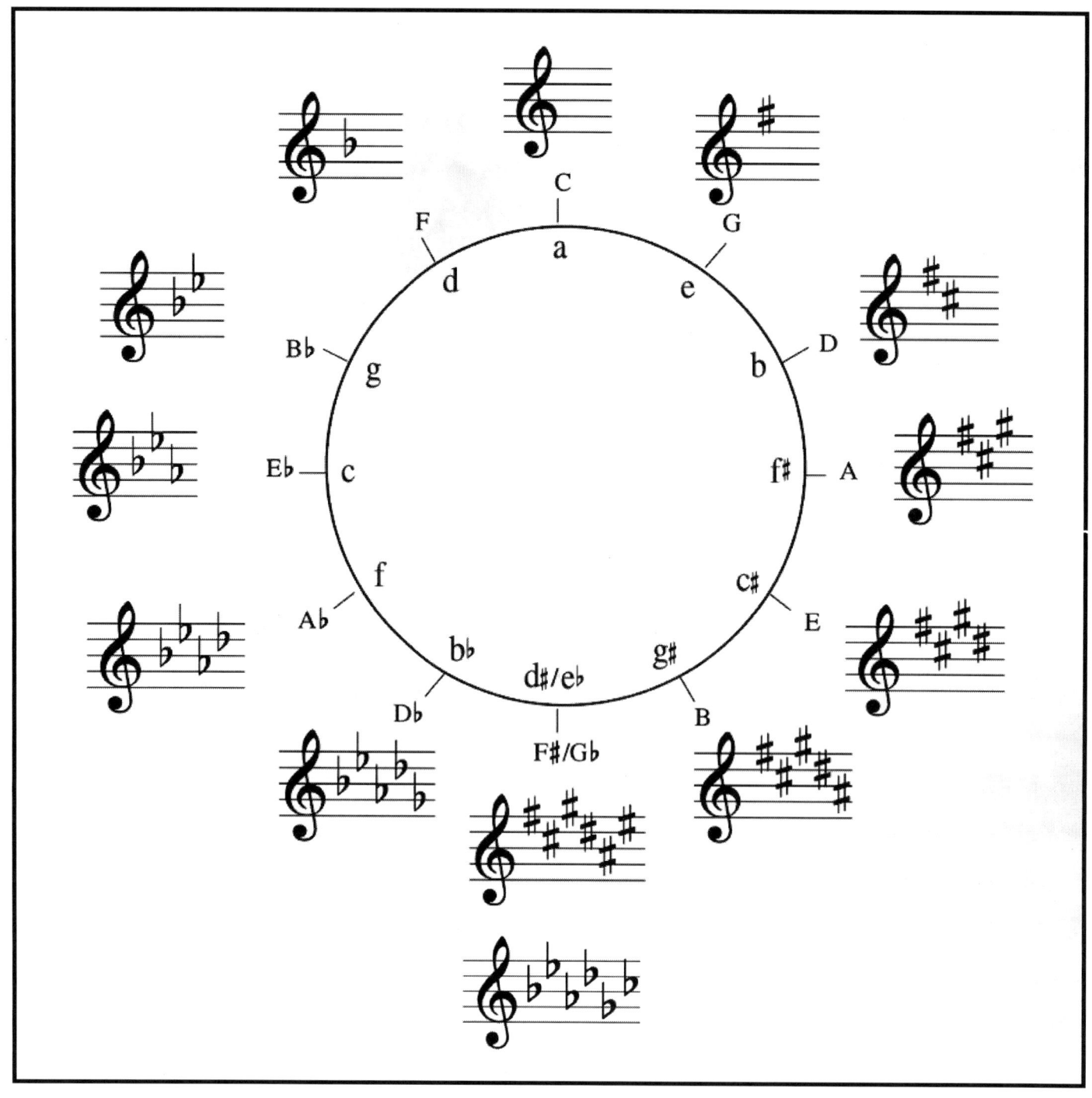

The lower-case letters inside the circle represent the key signatures' relative minor keys.

Major Scales

MAJOR KEY	1(TONIC)	2(9)	3	4(11)	5	6(13)	7	8
C major	C	D	E	F	G	A	B	C
G major	G	A	B	C	D	E	F#	G
D major	D	E	F#	G	A	B	C#	D
A major	A	B	C#	D	E	F#	G#	A
E major	E	F#	G#	A	B	C#	D#	E
B major	B	C#	D#	E	F#	G#	A#	B
F# major	F#	G#	A#	B	C#	D#	E#	F#
Gb major	Gb	Ab	Bb	Cb	Db	Eb	F	Gb
Db major	Db	Eb	F	Gb	Ab	Bb	C	Db
Ab major	Ab	Bb	C	Db	Eb	F	G	Ab
Eb major	Eb	F	G	Ab	Bb	C	D	Eb
Bb major	Bb	C	D	Eb	F	G	A	Bb
F major	F	G	A	Bb	C	D	E	F

Natural Minor Scales

MINOR KEY	1(TONIC)	2(9)	3	4(11)	5	6(13)	7	8
A minor	A	B	C	D	E	F	G	A
E minor	E	F#	G	A	B	C	D	E
B minor	B	C#	D	E	F#	G	A	B
F# minor	F#	G#	A	B	C#	D	E	F#
C# minor	C#	D#	E	F#	G#	A	B	C#
G# minor	G#	A#	B	C#	D#	E	F#	G#
D# minor	D#	E#	F#	G#	A#	B	C#	D#
Eb minor	Eb	F	Gb	Ab	Bb	Cb	Db	Eb
Bb minor	Bb	C	Db	Eb	F	Gb	Ab	Bb
F minor	F	G	Ab	Bb	C	Db	Eb	F
C minor	C	D	Eb	F	G	Ab	Bb	C
G minor	G	A	Bb	C	D	Eb	F	G
D minor	D	E	F	G	A	Bb	C	D

To create a harmonic minor scale, raise the 7th scale degree of the natural minor scale one half step.

To create a melodic minor scale, raise the 6th and 7th scale degrees of the natural minor scale one half step while ascending. The 6th and 7th degrees are not raised when descending.

The Harmonized Major Scales

KEYS	I	ii	iii	IV	V	vi	vii°
C major	C	Dm	Em	F	G	Am	B°
G major	G	Am	Bm	C	D	Em	F#°
D major	D	Em	F#m	G	A	Bm	C#°
A major	A	Bm	C#m	D	E	F#m	G#°
E major	E	F#m	G#m	A	B	C#m	D#°
B major	B	C#m	D#m	E	F#	G#m	A#°
F# major	F#	G#	A#m	B	C#	D#m	E#°
G♭ major	G♭	A♭m	B♭m	C♭	D♭	E♭m	F°
D♭ major	D♭	E♭m	Fm	G♭	A♭	B♭m	C°
A♭ major	A♭	B♭m	Cm	D♭	E♭	Fm	G°
E♭ major	E♭	Fm	Gm	A♭	B♭	Cm	D°
B♭ major	B♭	Cm	Dm	E♭	F	Gm	A°
F major	F	Gm	Am	B♭	C	Dm	E°

The Harmonized Natural Minor Scales

KEYS	i	ii°	III	iv	v	VI	VII
A minor	Am	B°	C	Dm	Em	F	G
E minor	Em	F#°	G	Am	Bm	C	D
B minor	Bm	C#°	D	Em	F#m	G	A
F# minor	F#m	G#°	A	Bm	C#m	D	E
C# minor	C#m	D#°	E	F#m	G#m	A	B
G# minor	G#m	A#°	B	C#m	D#m	E	F#
D# minor	D#m	E#°	F#	G#m	A#m	B	C#
E♭ minor	E♭mi	F°	G♭	A♭m	B♭m	C♭	D♭
B♭ minor	B♭m	C°	D♭	E♭m	Fm	G♭	A♭
F minor	Fm	G°	A♭	B♭m	Cm	D♭	E♭
C minor	Cm	D°	E♭	Fm	Gm	A♭	B♭
G minor	Gm	A°	B♭	Cm	Dm	E♭	F
D minor	Dm	E°	F	Gm	Am	B♭	C

Chord Construction

CHORD TYPE	FORMULA	NOTES	CHORD NAME
MAJOR	1-3-5	C-E-G	C
FIFTH (POWER CHORD)	1-5	C-G	C5
SUSPENDED FOURTH	1-4-5	C-F-G	Csus4
SUSPENDED SECOND	1-2-5	C-D-G	Csus2
ADDED NINTH	1-3-5-9	C-E-G-D	Cadd9
SIXTH	1-3-5-6	C-E-G-A	C6
SIXTH, ADDED NINTH	1-3-5-6-9	C-E-G-A-D	C6/9
MAJOR SEVENTH	1-3-5-7	C-E-G-B	Cmaj7
MAJOR NINTH	1-3-5-7-9	C-E-G-B-D	Cmaj9
MAJOR SEVENTH, SHARP ELEVENTH	1-3-5-7-#11	C-E-G-B-F#	Cmaj7#11
MAJOR THIRTEENTH	1-3-5-7-9-13	C-E-G-B-D-A	Cmaj13
MINOR	1-b3-5	C-Eb-G	Cm
MINOR, ADDED NINTH	1-b3-5-9	C-Eb-G-D	Cm(add9)
MINOR SIXTH	1-b3-5-6	C-Eb-G-A	Cm6
MINOR, FLAT SIXTH	1-b3-5-b6	C-Eb-G-Ab	Cmb6
MINOR SIXTH, ADDED NINTH	1-b3-5-6-9	C-Eb-G-A-D	Cm6/9
MINOR SEVENTH	1-b3-5-b7	C-Eb-G-Bb	Cm7
MINOR SEVENTH, FLAT FIFTH	1-b3-b5-b7	C-Eb-Gb-Bb	Cm7b5
MINOR, MAJOR SEVENTH	1-b3-5-7	C-Eb-G-B	Cm(maj7)
MINOR NINTH	1-b3-5-b7-9	C-Eb-G-Bb-D	Cm9
MINOR NINTH, FLAT FIFTH	1-b3-b5-b7-9	C-Eb-Gb-Bb-D	Cm9b5
MINOR NINTH, MAJOR SEVENTH	1-b3-5-7-9	C-Eb-G-B-D	Cm9maj7
MINOR ELEVENTH	1-b3-5-b7-9-11	C-Eb-G-Bb-D-F	Cm11
MINOR THIRTEENTH	1-b3-5-b7-9-11-13	C-Eb-G-Bb-D-F-A	Cm13
DOMINANT SEVENTH	1-3-5-b7	C-E-G-Bb	C7
SEVENTH, SUSPENDED FOURTH	1-4-5-b7	C-F-G-Bb	C7sus4
SEVENTH, FLAT FIFTH	1-3-b5-b7	C-E-Gb-Bb	C7b5
NINTH	1-3-5-b7-9	C-E-G-Bb-D	C9
NINTH, SUSPENDED FOURTH	1-4-5-b7-9	C-F-G-Bb-D	C9sus4
NINTH, FLAT FIFTH	1-3-b5-b7-9	C-E-Gb-Bb-D	C9b5
SEVENTH, FLAT NINTH	1-3-5-b7-b9	C-E-G-Bb-Db	C7b9
SEVENTH, SHARP NINTH	1-3-5-b7-#9	C-E-G-Bb-D#	C7#9
SEVENTH, FLAT FIFTH, SHARP NINTH	1-3-b5-b7-#9	C-E-Gb-Bb-D#	C7b5#9
ELEVENTH	1-5-b7-9-11	C-G-Bb-D-F	C11
SEVENTH, SHARP ELEVENTH	1-3-5-b7-#11	C-E-G-Bb-F#	C7#11
THIRTEENTH	1-3-5-b7-9-13	C-E-G-Bb-D-A	C13
THIRTEENTH, SUSPENDED FOURTH	1-4-5-b7-9-13	C-F-G-Bb-D-A	C13sus4
AUGMENTED	1-3-#5	C-E-G#	C+
SEVENTH, SHARP FIFTH	1-3-#5-b7	C-E-G#-Bb	C7#5
NINTH, SHARP FIFTH	1-3-#5-b7-9	C-E-G#-Bb-D	C9#5
SEVENTH, SHARP FIFTH, FLAT NINTH	1-3-#5-b7-b9	C-E-G#-Bb-Db	C7#5b9
SEVENTH, SHARP FIFTH, SHARP NINTH	1-3-#5-b7-#9	C-E-G#-Bb-D#	C7#5#9
DIMINISHED	1-b3-b5	C-Eb-Gb	C°
DIMINISHED SEVENTH	1-b3-b5-bb7	C-Eb-Gb-Bbb	C°7

Scale Construction

SCALE	FORMULA	INTERVAL STRUCTURE
MAJOR	1-2-3-4-5-6-7	W-W-H-W-W-W-H
NATURAL MINOR	1-2-♭3-4-5-♭6-♭7	W-H-W-W-H-W-W
MAJOR PENTATONIC	1-2-3-5-6	W-W-1½-W-1½
MINOR PENTATONIC	1-♭3-4-5-♭7	1½-W-W-1½-W
BLUES	1-♭3-4-♭5-5-♭7	1½-W-H-H-1½-W
MAJOR BLUES	1-2-♭3-3-4-♭5-5-6-♭7	W-H-H-H-H-H-W-H-W
MINOR BLUES	1-2-♭3-4-♭5-5-♭6-♭7	W-H-W-H-H-H-W-W
IONIAN MODE (major)	1-2-3-4-5-6-7	W-W-H-W-W-W-H
DORIAN MODE	1-2-♭3-4-5-6-♭7	W-H-W-W-W-H-W
PHRYGIAN MODE	1-♭2-♭3-4-5-♭6-♭7	H-W-W-W-H-W-W
LYDIAN MODE	1-2-3-♯4-5-6-7	W-W-W-H-W-W-H
MIXOLYDIAN MODE	1-2-3-4-5-6-♭7	W-W-H-W-W-H-W
AEOLIAN MODE (nat. minor)	1-2-♭3-4-5-♭6-♭7	W-H-W-W-H-W-W
LOCRIAN MODE	1-♭2-♭3-4-♭5-♭6-♭7	H-W-W-H-W-W-W
HARMONIC MINOR	1-2-♭3-4-5-♭6-7	W-H-W-W-H-1½-H
PHRYGIAN DOMINANT (Spanish)	1-♭2-3-4-5-♭6-♭7	H-1½-H-W-H-W-W
JAZZ MELODIC MINOR	1-2-♭3-4-5-6-7	W-H-W-W-W-W-H
DORIAN ♭2	1-♭2-♭3-4-5-6-♭7	H-W-W-W-W-H-W
LYDIAN AUGMENTED	1-2-3-♯4-♯5-6-7	W-W-W-W-H-W-H
LYDIAN ♭7	1-2-3-♯4-5-6-♭7	W-W-W-H-W-H-W
MIXOLYDIAN ♭13 (Hindu)	1-2-3-4-5-♭6-♭7	W-W-H-W-H-W-W
LOCRIAN ♯2	1-2-♭3-4-♭5-♭6-♭7	W-H-W-H-W-W-W
SUPER LOCRIAN (Altered)	1-♭2-♭3-♭4-♭5-♭6-♭7	H-W-H-W-W-W-W
CHROMATIC	1-♭2-2-♭3-3-4-♭5-5-♭6-6-♭7-7	H-H-H-H-H-H-H-H-H-H-H-H
WHOLE TONE	1-2-3-♯4-♯5-♯6	W-W-W-W-W-W
DIMINISHED WHOLE HALF	1-2-♭3-4-♭5-♭6-6-7	W-H-W-H-W-H-W-H
DIMINISHED HALF WHOLE	1-♭2-♭3-♭4-♭5-5-6-♭7	H-W-H-W-H-W-H-W
HUNGARIAN MINOR	1-2-♭3-♯4-5-♭6-7	W-H-1½-H-H-1½
DOUBLE HARMONIC	1-♭2-3-4-5-♭6-7	H-1½-H-W-H-1½-H
ENIGMATIC	1-♭2-3-♯4-♯5-♯6-7	H-1½-W-W-W-H-H
JAPANESE	1-♭2-4-5-♭6	H-2-W-H-2